# State of the Union Addresses of Thomas Jefferson

## 1801-1808

By Thomas Jefferson

# Contents

# State of the Union Address

## *December 8, 1801*

Fellow Citizens of the Senate and House of Representatives:

It is a circumstance of sincere gratification to me that on meeting the great council of our nation I am able to announce to them on grounds of reasonable certainty that the wars and troubles which have for so many years afflicted our sister nations have at length come to an end, and that the communications of peace and commerce are once more opening among them. Whilst we devoutly return thanks to the beneficent Being who has been pleased to breathe into them the spirit of conciliation and forgiveness, we are bound with peculiar gratitude to be thankful to Him that our own peace has been preserved through so perilous a season, and ourselves permitted quietly to cultivate the earth and to practice and improve those arts which tend to increase our comforts. The assurances, indeed, of friendly disposition received from all the powers with whom we have principle relations had inspired a confidence that our peace with them would not have been disturbed. But a cessation of irregularities which had affected the commerce of neutral nations and of the irritations and injuries produced by them can not but add to this confidence, and strengthens at the same time the hope that wrongs committed on unoffending friends under a pressure of circumstances will now be reviewed with candor, and will be considered as founding just claims of retribution for the past and new assurance for the future.

Among our Indian neighbors also a spirit of peace and friendship generally prevails, and I am happy to inform you that the continued efforts to introduce among them the implements and the practice of husbandry and the household arts have not been without success; that they are becoming more and more sensible of the superiority of this dependence for clothing and subsistence over the precarious resources of hunting and fishing, and already we are able to announce that instead of that constant diminution of their numbers produced by their wars and their wants, some of them begin to experience an increase of population.

To this state of general peace with which we have been blessed, one only exception exists. Tripoli, the least considerable of the Barbary States, had come forward with demands unfounded either in right or in compact, and had permitted itself to denounce war on our failure to comply before a given day. The style of the demand admitted but one answer.

I sent a small squadron of frigates into the Mediterranean, with assurances to that power of our sincere desire to remain in peace, but with orders to protect our commerce against the threatened attack. The measure was seasonable and salutary. The Bey had already declared war. His cruisers were out. Two had arrived at Gibraltar. Our commerce in the Mediterranean was blockaded and that of the Atlantic in peril.

The arrival of our squadron dispelled the danger. One of the Tripolitan cruisers having fallen in with and engaged the small schooner Enterprise, commanded by Lieutenant Sterret, which had gone as a tender to our larger vessels, was captured, after a heavy slaughter of her men, without the loss of a single one on our part. The bravery exhibited by our citizens on that element will, I trust, be a testimony to the world that it is not the want of that virtue which makes us seek their peace, but a conscientious desire to direct the energies of our nation to the multiplication of the human race, and not to its destruction. Unauthorized by the Constitution, without the sanction of Congress, to go beyond the line of defense, the vessel, being disabled from committing further hostilities, was liberated with its crew.

The Legislature will doubtless consider whether, by authorizing measures of offense also, they will place our force on an equal footing with that of its adversaries. I communicate all material information on this subject, that in the exercise of this important function confided by the Constitution to the Legislature exclusively their judgment may form itself on a knowledge and consideration of every circumstance of weight.

I wish I could say that our situation with all the other Barbary States was entirely satisfactory. Discovering that some delays had taken place in the performance of certain articles stipulated by us, I thought it my duty, by immediate measures for fulfilling them, to vindicate to ourselves the right of considering the effect of departure from stipulation on their side. From the papers which will be laid before you you will be enabled to judge whether our treaties are regarded by them as fixing at all the measure of their demands or as guarding from the exercise of force our vessels within their power, and to consider how far it will be safe and expedient to leave our affairs with them in their present posture.

I lay before you the result of the census lately taken of our inhabitants, to a conformity with which we are now to reduce the ensuing ration of representation and taxation. You will perceive that the increase of numbers during the last 10 years, proceeding in geometric ratio, promises a duplication in little more than 22 years. We contemplate this rapid growth and the prospect it holds up to us, not with a view to the injuries it may enable us to do others in some future day, but to the settlement of the extensive country still remaining vacant within our limits to the multiplication of men susceptible of happiness, educated in the love of order, habituated to self-government, and valuing its blessings above all price.

Other circumstances, combined with the increase of numbers, have produced an augmentation of revenue arising from consumption in a ratio far beyond that of population alone; and though the changes in foreign relations now taking place so desirably for the whole world may for a season affect this branch of revenue, yet weighing all probabilities of expense as well as of income, there is reasonable ground of confidence that we may now safely dispense with all the internal taxes, comprehending excise, stamps, auctions, licenses, carriages, and refined sugars, to which the postage on news papers may be added to facilitate the progress of information, and that the remaining sources of revenue will be sufficient to provide for the support of Government, to pay the interest of the public debts, and to discharge the principals within shorter periods than the laws or the general expectation had contemplated.

War, indeed, and untoward events may change this prospect of things and call for expenses which imposts could not meet; but sound principles will not justify our taxing the industry of our fellow citizens to accumulate treasure for wars to happen we know not when, and which might not, perhaps, happen but from the temptations offered by that treasure.

These views, however, of reducing our burthens are formed on the expectation that a sensible and at the same time a salutary reduction may take place in our habitual expenditures. For this purpose those of the civil Government, the Army, and Navy will need revisal.

When we consider that this Government is charged with the external and mutual relations only of these States; that the States themselves have principal care of our persons, our property, and our reputation, constituting the great field of human concerns, we may well doubt whether our organization is not too complicated, too expensive; whether offices and officers have not been multiplied unnecessarily and sometimes injuriously to the service they were meant to promote.

I will cause to be laid before you an essay toward a statement of those who, under public employment of various kinds, draw money from the Treasury or from our citizens. Time has not permitted a perfect enumeration, the ramifications of office being too multiplied and remote to be completely traced in a first trial.

Among those who are dependent on Executive discretion I have begun the reduction of what was deemed unnecessary. The expenses of diplomatic agency have been considerably diminished. The inspectors of internal revenue who were found to obstruct the accountability of the institution have been discontinued. Several agencies created by Executive authorities, on salaries fixed by that also, have been suppressed, and should suggest the expediency of regulating that power by law, so as to subject its exercises to legislative inspection and sanction.

Other reformations of the same kind will be pursued with that caution which is requisite in removing useless things, not to injure what is retained. But the great mass of public offices is established by law, and therefore by law alone can be abolished. Should the Legislature think it expedient to pass this roll in review and try all its parts by the test of public utility, they may be assured of every aid and light which Executive information can yield.

Considering the general tendency to multiply offices and dependencies and to increase expense to the ultimate term of burthen which the citizen can bear, it behooves us to avail ourselves of every occasion which presents itself for taking off the surcharge, that it never may be seen here that after leaving to labor the smallest portion of its earnings on which it can subsist, Government shall itself consume the whole residue of what it was instituted to guard.

In our care, too, of the public contributions intrusted to our direction it would be prudent to multiply barriers against their dissipation by appropriating specific sums to every specific purpose susceptible of definition; by disallowing all applications of money varying from the appropriation in object or transcending it in amount; by reducing the undefined field of contingencies and thereby circumscribing discretionary powers over money, and by bringing back to a single department all accountabilities for money, where the examinations may be prompt, efficacious, and uniform.

An account of the receipts and expenditures of the last year, as prepared by the Secretary of the Treasury, will, as usual, be laid before you. The success which has attended the late sales of the public lands shews that with attention they may be made an important source of receipt. Among the payments those made in discharge of the principal and interest of the national debt will shew that the public faith has been exactly maintained. To these will be added an estimate of appropriations necessary for the ensuing year.

This last will, of course, be affected by such modifications of the system of expense as you shall think proper to adopt.

A statement has been formed by the Secretary of War, on mature consideration, of all the posts and stations where garrisons will be expedient and of the number of men requisite for each garrison. The whole amount is considerably short of the present military establishment. For the surplus no particular use can be pointed out.

For defense against invasion their number is as nothing, nor is it conceived needful or safe that a standing army should be kept up in time of peace for that purpose. Uncertain as we must ever be of the particular point in our circumference where an enemy may choose to invade us, the only force which can be ready at every point and competent to oppose them is the body of the neighboring citizens as formed into a militia. On these, collected from the parts most convenient in numbers proportioned to the invading force, it is best to rely not only to meet the first attack, but if it threatens to be permanent to maintain the defense until regulars may be engaged to relieve them. These considerations render it important that we should at every session continue to amend the defects which from time to time shew themselves in the laws for regulating the militia until they are sufficiently perfect. Nor should we now or at any time separate until we say we have done everything for the militia which we could do were an enemy at our door.

The provision of military stores on hand will be laid before you, that you may judge of the additions still requisite.

With respect to the extent to which our naval preparations should be expected to appear, but just attention to the circumstances of every part of the Union will doubtless reconcile all. A small force will probably continue to be wanted for actual service in the Mediterranean. Whatever annual sum beyond that you may think proper to appropriate to naval preparations would perhaps be better employed in providing those articles which may be kept without waste or consumption, and be in readiness when any exigence calls them into use. Progress has been made, as will appear by papers now communicated, in providing materials for 74-gun ships as directed by law.

How far the authority given by the Legislature for procuring and establishing sites for naval purposes has been perfectly understood and pursued in the execution admits of some doubt. A statement of the expenses already incurred on that subject is now laid before you. I have in certain cases suspended or slackened these expenditures, that the Legislature might determine whether so many yards are necessary as have been contemplated.

The works at this place are among those permitted to go on, and 5 of the 7 frigates directed to be laid up have been brought and laid up here, where, besides the safety of their position, they are under the eye of the Executive Administration, as well as of its agents, and where yourselves also will be guided by your own view in the legislative provisions respecting them which may from time to time be necessary. They are preserved in such condition, as well the vessels as whatever belongs to them, as to be at all times ready for sea on a short warning. Two others are yet to be laid up so soon as they shall have received the repairs requisite to put them also into sound condition. As a superintending officer will be necessary at each yard, his duties and emoluments, hitherto fixed by the Executive, will be a more proper subject for legislation. A communication will also be made of our progress in the execution of the law respecting the vessels directed to be sold.

The fortifications of our harbors, more or less advanced, present considerations of great difficulty. While some of them are on a scale sufficiently proportioned to the advantages of their position, to the efficacy of their protection, and the importance of the points within it, others are so extensive, will cost so much in their first erection, so much in their maintenance, and require such a force to garrison them as to make it questionable what is best now to be done. A statement of those commenced or projected, of the expenses already incurred, and estimates of their future cost, as far as can be foreseen, shall be laid before you, that you may be enabled to judge whether any alteration is necessary in the laws respecting this subject.

Agriculture, manufactures, commerce, and navigation, the four pillars of our prosperity, are then most thriving when left most free to individual enterprise. Protection from casual embarrassments, however, may sometimes be seasonably interposed. If in the course of your observations or inquiries they should appear to need any aid within the limits of our constitutional powers, your sense of their importance is a sufficient assurance they will occupy your attention. We can not, indeed, but all feel an anxious solicitude for the difficulties under which our carrying trade will soon be placed. How far it can be relieved, otherwise than by time, is a subject of important consideration.

The judiciary system of the United States, and especially that portion of it recently erected, will of course present itself to the contemplation of Congress, and, that they may be able to judge of the proportion which the institution bears on the business it has to perform, I have caused to be procured from the several States and now lay before

Congress an exact statement of all the causes decided since the first establishment of the courts, and of those which were depending when additional courts and judges were brought in to their aid.

And while on the judiciary organization it will be worthy your consideration whether the protection of the inestimable institution of juries has been extended to all the cases involving the security of our persons and property. Their impartial selection also being essential to their value, we ought further to consider whether that is sufficiently secured in those States where they are named by a marshal depending on Executive will or designated by the court or by officers dependent on them.

I can not omit recommending a revisal of the laws on the subject of naturalization. Considering the ordinary chances of human life, a denial of citizenship under a residence of 14 years is a denial to a great proportion of those who ask it, and controls a policy pursued from their first settlement by many of these States, and still believed of consequence to their prosperity; and shall we refuse to the unhappy fugitives from distress that hospitality which the savages of the wilderness extended to our fathers arriving in this land? Shall oppressed humanity find no asylum on this globe? The Constitution indeed has wisely provided that for admission to certain offices of important trust a residence shall be required sufficient to develop character and design. But might not the general character and capabilities of a citizen be safely communicated to everyone manifesting a bona fide purpose of embarking his life and fortunes permanently with us, with restrictions, perhaps, to guard against the fraudulent usurpation of our flag, an abuse which brings so much embarrassment and loss on the genuine citizen and so much danger to the nation of being involved in war that no endeavor should be spared to detect and suppress it?

These, fellow citizens, are the matters respecting the state of the nation which I have thought of importance to be submitted to your consideration at this time. Some others of less moment or not yet ready for communication will be the subject of separate messages. I am happy in this opportunity of committing the arduous affairs of our Government to the collected wisdom of the Union. Nothing shall be wanting on my part to inform as far as in my power the legislative judgment, nor to carry that judgment into faithful execution.

The prudence and temperance of your discussions will promote within your own walls that conciliation which so much befriends rational conclusion, and by its example will encourage among our constituents that progress of opinion which is tending to unite them in object and in will. That all should be satisfied with any one order of things is not to be expected; but I indulge the pleasing persuasion that the great body of our citizens will cordially concur in honest and disinterested efforts which have for their object to preserve the General and State Governments in their constitutional form and equilibrium; to maintain peace abroad, and order and obedience to the laws at home; to establish principles and practices of administration favorable to the security of liberty and property, and to reduce expenses to what is necessary for the useful purposes of Government.

# State of the Union Address

## *December 15, 1802*

To the Senate and House of Representatives:

When we assemble together, fellow citizens, to consider the state of our beloved country, our just attentions are first drawn to those pleasing circumstances which mark the goodness of that Being from whose favor they flow and the large measure of thankfulness we owe for His bounty. Another year has come around, and finds us still blessed with peace and friendship abroad; law, order, and religion at home; good affection and harmony with our Indian neighbors; our burthens lightened, yet our income sufficient for the public wants, and the produce of the year great beyond example. These, fellow citizens, are the circumstances under which we meet, and we remark with special satisfaction those which under the smiles of Providence result from the skill, industry, and order of our citizens, managing their own affairs in their own way and for their own use, unembarrassed by too much regulation, unoppressed by fiscal exactions.

On the restoration of peace in Europe that portion of the general carrying trade which had fallen to our share during the war was abridged by the returning competition of the belligerent powers. This was to be expected, and was just. But in addition we find in some parts of Europe monopolizing discriminations, which in the form of duties tend effectually to prohibit the carrying thither our own produce in our own vessels. From existing amities and a spirit of justice it is hoped that friendly discussion will produce a fair and adequate reciprocity. But should false calculations of interest defeat our hope, it rests with the

Legislature to decide whether they will meet inequalities abroad with countervailing inequalities at home, or provide for the evil in any other way.

It is with satisfaction I lay before you an act of the British Parliament anticipating this subject so far as to authorize a mutual abolition of the duties and countervailing duties permitted under the treaty of 1794. It shows on their part a spirit of justice and friendly accommodation which it is our duty and our interest to cultivate with all nations. Whether this would produce a due equality in the navigation between the two countries is a subject for your consideration.

Another circumstance which claims attention as directly affecting the very source of our navigation is the defect or the evasion of the law providing for the return of sea men, and particularly of those belonging to vessels sold abroad. Numbers of them, discharged in foreign ports, have been thrown on the hands of our consuls, who, to rescue them from the dangers into which their distresses might plunge them and save them to their country, have found it necessary in some cases to return them at the public charge.

The cession of the Spanish Province of Louisiana to France, which took place in the course of the late war, will, if carried into effect, make a change in the aspect of our foreign relations which will doubtless have just weight in any deliberations of the Legislature connected with that subject.

There was reason not long since to apprehend that the warfare in which we were engaged with Tripoli might be taken up by some other of the Barbary Powers. A reenforcement, therefore, was immediately ordered to the vessels already there. Subsequent information, however, has removed these apprehensions for the present. To secure our commerce in that sea with the smallest force competent, we have supposed it best to watch strictly the harbor of Tripoli. Still, however, the shallowness of their coast and the want of smaller vessels on our part has permitted some cruisers to escape unobserved, and to one of these an American vessel unfortunately fell prey. The captain, one American sea man, and two others of color remain prisoners with them unless exchanged under an agreement formerly made with the Bashaw, to whom, on the faith of that, some of his captive subjects had been restored.

The convention with the State of Georgia has been ratified by their legislature, and a repurchase from the Creeks has been consequently made of a part of the Talasscee country. In this purchase has been also comprehended a part of the lands within the fork of Oconee and Oakmulgee rivers. The particulars of the contract will be laid before Congress so soon as they shall be in a state for communication.

In order to remove every ground of difference possible with our Indian neighbors, I have proceeded in the work of settling with them and marking the boundaries between us. That with the Choctaw Nation is fixed in one part and will be through the whole within a short time. The country to which their title had been extinguished before the Revolution is sufficient to receive a very respectable population, which Congress will probably see the expediency of encouraging so soon as the limits shall be declared. We are to view this position as an outpost of the United States, surrounded by strong neighbors and distant from its support; and how far that monopoly which prevents population should here be guarded against and actual habitation made a condition of the continuance of title will be for your consideration. A prompt settlement, too, of all existing rights and claims within this territory presents itself as a preliminary operation.

In that part of the Indiana Territory which includes Vincennes the lines settled with the neighboring tribes fix the extinction of their title at a breadth of 24 leagues from east to west and about the same length parallel with and including the Wabash. They have also ceded a tract of 4 miles square, including the salt springs near the mouth of that river.

In the Department of Finance it is with pleasure I inform you, that the receipts of external duties for the last 12 months have exceeded those of any former year, and that the ration of increase has been also greater than usual. This has enabled us to answer all the regular exigencies of Government, to pay from the Treasury within one year upward of $8 millions, principal and interest, of the public debt, exclusive of upward of $1 million paid by the sale of bank stock, and making in the whole a reduction of nearly $5.5 millions of principal, and to have now in the Treasury $4.5 millions which are in a course of application to the further discharge of debt and current demands. Experience, too, so far, authorizes us to believe, if no extraordinary event supervenes, and the expenses which will be actually incurred shall not be greater than were contemplated by Congress at their last session, that we shall not be disappointed in the expectations then formed. But nevertheless, as the effect of peace on the amount of duties is not yet fully ascertained, it is the more necessary to practice every useful economy and to incur no expense which may be avoided without prejudice.

The collection of the internal taxes having been completed in some of the States, the officers employed in it are of course out of commission. In others they will be so shortly.

But in a few, where the arrangements for the direct tax had been retarded, it will be some time before the system is closed. It has not yet been thought necessary to employ the agent authorized by an act of the last session for transacting business in Europe relative to debts and loans. Nor have we used the power confided by the same act of prolonging the foreign debt by reloans, and of redeeming instead thereof an equal sum of the domestic debt. Should, however, the difficulties of remittance on so large a scale render it necessary at any time, the power shall be executed and the money thus employed abroad shall, in conformity with that law, be faithfully applied here in an equivalent extinction of domestic debt.

When effects so salutary result from the plans you have already sanctioned; when merely by avoiding false objects of expense we are able, without a direct tax, without internal taxes, and without borrowing to make large and effectual payments toward the discharge of our public debt and the emancipation of our posterity from that mortal canker, it is an encouragement, fellow citizens, of the highest order to proceed as we have begun in substituting economy for taxation, and in pursuing what is useful for a nation placed as we are, rather than what is practiced by others under different circumstances. And when so ever we are destined to meet events which shall call forth all the energies of our country-men, we have the firmest reliance on those energies and the comfort of leaving for calls like these the extraordinary resources of loans and internal taxes. In the mean time, by payments of the principal of our debt, we are liberating annually portions of the external taxes and forming from them a growing fund still further to lessen the necessity of recurring to extraordinary resources. The usual account of receipts and expenditures for the last year, with an estimate of the expenses of the ensuing one, will be laid before you by the Secretary of the Treasury.

No change being deemed necessary in our military establishment, an estimate of its expenses for the ensuing year on its present footing, as also of the sums to be employed in fortifications and other objects within that department, has been prepared by the Secretary of War, and will make a part of the general estimates which will be presented you.

Considering that our regular troops are employed for local purposes, and that the militia is our general reliance for great and sudden emergencies, you will doubtless think this institution worthy of a review, and give it those improvements of which you find it susceptible.

Estimates for the Naval Department, prepared by the Secretary of the Navy, for another year will in like manner be communicated with the general estimates. A small force in the Mediterranean will still be necessary to restrain the Tripoline cruisers, and the uncertain tenure of peace with some other of the Barbary Powers may eventually require that force to be augmented. The necessity of procuring some smaller vessels for that service will raise the estimate, but the difference in their maintenance will soon make it a measure of economy.

Presuming it will be deemed expedient to expend annually a convenient sum toward providing the naval defense which our situation may require, I can not but recommend that the first appropriations for that purpose may go to the saving what we already possess. No cares, no attentions, can preserve vessels from rapid decay which lie in water and exposed to the sun. These decays require great and constant repairs, and will consume, if continued, a great portion of the moneys destined to naval purposes. To avoid this waste of our resources it is proposed to add to our navy-yard here a dock within which our present vessels may be laid up dry and under cover from the sun. Under these circumstances experience proves that works of wood will remain scarcely at all affected by time. The great abundance of running water which this situation possesses, at heights far above the level of the tide, if employed as is practiced for lock navigation, furnishes the means for raising and laying up our vessels on a dry and sheltered bed. And should the measure be found useful here, similar depositories for laying up as well as for building and repairing vessels may hereafter be undertaken at other navy-yards offering the same means. The plans and estimates of the work, prepared by a person of skill and experience, will be presented to you without delay, and from this it will be seen that scarcely more than has been the cost of one vessel is necessary to save the whole, and that the annual sum to be employed toward its completion may be adapted to the views of the Legislature as to naval expenditure. To cultivate peace and maintain commerce and navigation in all their lawful enterprises; to foster our fisheries as nurseries of navigation and for the nurture of man, and protect the manufactures adapted to our circumstances; to preserve the faith of the nation by an exact discharge of its debts and contracts, expend the public money with the same care and economy we would practice with our own, and impose on our citizens no unnecessary burthens; to keep in all things within the pale of our constitutional powers, and cherish the federal union as the only rock of safety—these, fellow citizens, are the land-marks by which we are to guide ourselves in all proceedings. By continuing to make these the rule of our action we shall endear to our country-men the true principles of their Constitution and promote an union of sentiment and of action equally auspicious to their happiness and safety. On my part, you may count on a cordial concurrence in every measure for the public good and on all the information I possess which may enable you to discharge to advantage the high functions with which you are invested by your country.

TH. JEFFERSON

# State of the Union Address

## *October 17, 1803*

To The Senate and House of Representatives of the United States:

In calling you together, fellow citizens, at an earlier day than was contemplated by the act of the last session of Congress, I have not been insensible to the personal inconveniences necessarily resulting from an unexpected change in your arrangements, but matters of great public concernment have rendered this call necessary, and the interests you feel in these will supersede in your minds all private considerations.

Congress witnessed at their late session the extraordinary agitation produced in the public mind by the suspension of our right of deposit at the port of New Orleans, no assignment of another place having been made according to treaty. They were sensible that the continuance of that privation would be more injurious to our nation than any consequences which could flow from any mode of redress, but reposing just confidence in the good faith of the Government whose officer had committed the wrong, friendly and reasonable representations were resorted to, and the right of deposit was restored.

Previous, however, to this period we had not been unaware of the danger to which our peace would be perpetually exposed whilst so important a key to the commerce of the Western country remained under foreign power. Difficulties, too, were presenting themselves as to the navigation of other streams which, arising within our territories, pass through those adjacent. Propositions had therefore been authorized for obtaining on fair conditions the sovereignty of New Orleans and of other possessions in that quarter interesting to our quiet to such extent as was deemed practicable, and the provisional appropriation of $2 millions to be applied and accounted for by the President of the United States, intended as part of the price, was considered as conveying the sanction of Congress to the acquisition proposed. The enlightened Government of France saw with just discernment the importance to both nations of such liberal arrangements as might best and permanently promote the peace, friendship, and interests of both, and the property and sovereignty of all Louisiana which had been restored to them have on certain conditions been transferred to the United States by instruments bearing date the 30th of April last. When these shall have received the constitutional sanction of the Senate, they will without delay be communicated to the Representatives also for the exercise of their functions as to those conditions which are within the powers vested by the Constitution in Congress.

Whilst the property and sovereignty of the Mississippi and its waters secure an independent outlet for the produce of the Western States and an uncontrolled navigation through their whole course, free from collision with other powers and the dangers to our peace from that source, the fertility of the country, its climate and extent, promise in due season important aids to our Treasury, an ample provision for our posterity, and a wide spread for the blessings of freedom and equal laws.

With the wisdom of Congress it will rest to take those ulterior measures which may be necessary for the immediate occupation and temporary government of the country; for its incorporation into our Union; for rendering the change of government a blessing to our newly adopted brethren; for securing to them the rights of conscience and of property; for confirming to the Indian inhabitants their occupancy and self-government, establishing friendly and commercial relations with them, and for ascertaining the geography of the country acquired. Such materials, for your information, relative to its affairs in general as the short space of time has permitted me to collect will be laid before you when the subject shall be in a state for your consideration.

Another important acquisition of territory has also been made since the last session of Congress. The friendly tribe of Kaskaskia Indians, with which we have never had a difference, reduced by the wars and wants of savage life to a few individuals unable to defend themselves against the neighboring tribes, has transferred its country to the United States, reserving only for its members what is sufficient to maintain them in an agricultural way. The considerations stipulated are that we shall extend to them our patronage and protection and give them certain annual aids in money, in implements of agriculture, and other articles of their choice. This country, among the most fertile within our limits, extending along the Mississippi from the mouth of the Illinois to and up to the Ohio, though not so necessary as a barrier since the acquisition of the other bank, may yet be well worthy of being laid open to immediate settlement, as its inhabitants may descend with rapidity in support of the lower country should future circumstances expose that to foreign enterprise. As the stipulations in this treaty involve matters with the competence of both Houses only, it will be laid before Congress as soon as the Senate shall have advised its ratification.

With many of the other Indian tribes improvements in agriculture and household manufacture are advancing, and with all our peace and friendship are established on grounds much firmer than heretofore. The measure adopted of establishing trading houses among them and of furnishing them necessaries in exchange for their commodities at such moderate prices as leave no gain, but cover us from loss, has the most conciliatory and useful effect on them, and is that which will best secure their peace and good will.

The small vessels authorized by Congress with a view to the Mediterranean service have been sent into that sea, and will be able more effectually to confine the Tripoline cruisers within their harbors and supersede the necessity of convoy to our commerce in that quarter. They will sensibly lessen the expenses of that service the ensuing year.

A further knowledge of the ground in the northeastern and northwestern angles of the United States has evinced that the boundaries established by the treaty of Paris between the British territories and ours in those parts were too imperfectly described to be susceptible of execution. It has therefore been thought worthy of attention for preserving and cherishing the harmony and useful intercourse subsisting between the two nations to remove by timely arrangements what unfavorable incidents might otherwise render a ground of future misunderstanding. A convention has therefore been entered into which provides for a practicable demarcation of those limits to the satisfaction of both parties.

An account of the receipts and expenditures of the year ending the 30th of September last, with the estimates for the service of the ensuing year, will be laid before you by the Secretary of the Treasury so soon as the receipts of the last quarter shall be returned from the more distant States. It is already ascertained that the amount paid into the Treasury for that year has been between $11 millions and $12 millions, and that the revenue accrued during the same term exceeds the sum counted on as sufficient for our current expenses and to extinguish the public debt within the period heretofore proposed.

The amount of debt paid for the same year is about $3.1 millions exclusive of interest, and making, with the payment of the preceding year, a discharge of more than $8.5 millions of the principal of that debt, besides the accruing interest; and there remain in the Treasury nearly $6 millions. Of these, $880 thousands have been reserved for payment of the first installment due under the British convention of January 8th, 1802, and $2 millions are what have been before mentioned as placed by Congress under the power and accountability of the President toward the price of New Orleans and other territories acquired, which, remaining untouched, are still applicable to that object and go in diminution of the sum to be funded for it.

Should the acquisition of Louisiana be constitutionally confirmed and carried into effect, a sum of nearly $13 millions will then be added to our public debt, most of which is payable after fifteen years, before which term the present existing debts will all be discharged by the established operation of the sinking fund. When we contemplate the ordinary annual augmentation of impost from increasing population and wealth, the augmentation of the same revenue by its extension to the new acquisition, and the economies which may still be introduced into our public expenditures, I can not but hope that Congress in reviewing their resources will find means to meet the intermediate interest of this additional debt without recurring to new taxes, and applying to this object only the ordinary progression of our revenue. Its extraordinary increase in times of foreign war will be the proper and sufficient fund for any measures of safety or precaution which that state of things may render necessary in our neutral position.

Remittances for the installments of our foreign debt having been found practicable without loss, it has not been thought expedient to use the power given by a former act of Congress of continuing them by reloans, and of redeeming instead thereof equal sums of domestic debt, although no difficulty was found in obtaining that accommodation.

The sum of $50 thousands appropriated by Congress for providing gun boats remains unexpended. The favorable and peaceable turn of affairs on the Mississippi rendered an immediate execution of that law unnecessary, and time was desirable in order that the institution of that branch of our force might begin on models the most approved by experience. The same issue of events dispensed with a resort to the appropriation of $1.5 millions, contemplated for purposes which were effected by happier means.

We have seen with sincere concern the flames of war lighted up again in Europe, and nations with which we have the most friendly and useful relations engaged in mutual destruction. While we regret the miseries in which we see others involved, let us bow with gratitude to that kind Providence which, inspiring with wisdom and moderation our late legislative councils while placed under the urgency of the greatest wrongs guarded us from hastily entering into the sanguinary contest and left us only to look on and pity its ravages.

These will be heaviest on those immediately engaged. Yet the nations pursuing peace will not be exempt from all evil.

In the course of this conflict let it be our endeavor, as it is our interest and desire, to cultivate the friendship of the belligerent nations by every act of justice and of innocent kindness; to receive their armed vessels with hospitality from the distresses of the sea, but to administer the means of annoyance to none; to establish in our harbors such a police as may maintain law and order; to restrain our citizens from embarking individually in a war in which their country takes no part; to punish severely those persons, citizens or alien, who shall usurp the cover of our flag for vessels not entitled to it, infecting thereby with suspicion those of real Americans and committing us into controversies for the redress of wrongs not our own; to exact from every nation the observance toward our vessels and citizens of those principles and practices which all civilized people acknowledge; to merit the character of a just nation, and maintain that of an independent one, preferring every consequence to insult and habitual wrong. Congress will consider whether the existing laws enable us efficaciously to maintain this course with our citizens in all places and with others while within the limits of our jurisdiction, and will give them the new modifications necessary for these objects. Some contraventions of right have already taken place, both within our jurisdictional limits and on the high seas. The friendly disposition of the Governments from whose agents they have proceeded, as well as their wisdom and regard for justice, leave us in reasonable expectation that they will be rectified and prevented in future, and that no act will be countenanced by them which threatens to disturb our friendly intercourse.

Separated by a wide ocean from the nations of Europe and from the political interests which entangle them together, with productions and wants which render our commerce and friendship useful to them and theirs to us, it can not be the interest of any to assail us, nor ours to disturb them. We should be most unwise, indeed, were we to cast away the singular blessings of the position in which nature has placed us, the opportunity she has endowed us with of pursuing, at a distance from foreign contentions, the paths of industry, peace, and happiness, of cultivating general friendship, and of bringing collisions of interest to the umpirage of reason rather than of force.

How desirable, then, must it be in a Government like ours to see its citizens adopt individually the views, the interests, and the conduct which their country should pursue, divesting themselves of those passions and partialities which tend to lessen useful friendships and to embarrass and embroil us in the calamitous scenes of Europe. Confident, fellow citizens, that you will duly estimate the importance of neutral dispositions toward the observance of neutral conduct, that you will be sensible how much it is our duty to look on the bloody arena spread before us with commiseration indeed, but with no other wish than to see it closed, I am persuaded you will cordially cherish these dispositions in all discussions among yourselves and in all communications with your constituents; and I anticipate with satisfaction the measures of wisdom which the great interests now committed to you will give you an opportunity of providing, and myself that of approving and carrying into execution with the fidelity I owe to my country.

TH. JEFFERSON

# State of the Union Address

## *November 8, 1804*

The Senate and House of Representatives of the United States:

To a people, fellow citizens, who sincerely desire the happiness and prosperity of other nations; to those who justly calculate that their own well-being is advanced by that of the nations with which they have intercourse, it will be a satisfaction to observe that the war which was lighted up in Europe a little before our last meeting has not yet extended its flames to other nations, nor been marked by the calamities which sometimes stain the foot-steps of war. The irregularities, too, on the ocean, which generally harass the commerce of neutral nations, have, in distant parts, disturbed ours less than on former occasions; but in the American seas they have been greater from peculiar causes, and even within our harbors and jurisdiction infringements on the authority of the laws have been committed which have called for serious attention. The friendly conduct of the Governments from whose officers and subjects these acts have proceeded, in other respects and in places more under their observation and control, gives us confidence that our representations on this subject will have been properly regarded.

While noticing the irregularities committed on the ocean by others, those on our own part should not be omitted nor left unprovided for. Complaints have been received that persons residing within the United States have taken on themselves to arm merchant vessels and to force a commerce into certain ports and countries in defiance of the laws of those countries. That individuals should undertake to wage private war, independently of the authority of their country, can not be permitted in a well-ordered society. Its tendency to produce aggression on the laws and rights of other nations and to endanger the peace of our own is so obvious that I doubt not you will adopt measures for restraining it effectually in future.

Soon after the passage of the act of the last session authorizing the establishment of a district and port of entry on the waters of the Mobile we learnt that its object was misunderstood on the part of Spain. Candid explanations were immediately given and assurances that, reserving our claims in that quarter as a subject of discussion and arrangement with Spain, no act was meditated in the mean time inconsistent with the peace and friendship existing between the two nations, and that conformably to these intentions would be the execution of the law. That Government had, however, thought proper to suspend the ratification of the convention of 1802; but the explanations which would reach them soon after, and still more the confirmation of them by the tenor of the instrument establishing the port and district, may reasonably be expected to replace them in the dispositions and views of the whole subject which originally dictated the convention.

I have the satisfaction to inform you that the objections which had been urged by that Government against the validity of our title to the country of Louisiana have been withdrawn, its exact limits, however, remaining still to be settled between us; and to this is to be added that, having prepared and delivered the stock created in execution of the convention of Paris of April 30th, 1803, in consideration of the cession of that country, we have received from the Government of France an acknowledgment, in due form, of the fulfillment of that stipulation.

With the nations of Europe in general our friendship and intercourse are undisturbed, and from the Governments of the belligerent powers especially we continue to receive those friendly manifestations which are justly due to an honest neutrality and to such good offices consistent with that as we have opportunities of rendering.

The activity and success of the small force employed in the Mediterranean in the early part of the present year, the reenforcements sent into that sea, and the energy of the officers having command in the several vessels will, I trust, by the sufferings of war, reduce the barbarians of Tripoli to the desire of peace on proper terms. Great injury, however, ensues to ourselves, as well as to others interested, from the distance to which prizes must be brought for adjudication and from the impracticability of bringing hither such as are not sea worthy.

The Bey of Tunis having made requisitions unauthorized by our treaty, their rejection has produced from him some expressions of discontent, but to those who expect us to calculate whether a compliance with unjust demands will not cost us less than a war we must leave as a question of calculation for them also whether to retire from unjust demands will not cost them less than a war. We can do to each other very sensible injuries by war, but the mutual advantages of peace make that the best interest of both.

Peace and intercourse with the other powers on the same coast continue on the footing on which they are established by treaty.

In pursuance of the act providing for the temporary government of Louisiana, the necessary officers for the Territory of Orleans were appointed in due time to commence the exercise of their functions on the first day of

October. The distance, however, of some of them and indispensable previous arrangements may have retarded its commencement in some of its parts. The form of government thus provided having been considered but as temporary, and open to such future improvements as further information of the circumstances of our brethren there might suggest, it will of course be subject to your consideration.

In the district of Louisiana it has been thought best to adopt the division into subordinate districts which had been established under its former government. These being five in number, a commanding officer has been appointed to each, according to the provisions of the law, and so soon as they can be at their stations that district will also be in its due state of organization. In the mean time, their places are supplied by the officers before commanding there, and the function of the governor and judges of Indiana having commenced, the government, we presume, is proceeding in its new form. The lead mines in that district offer so rich a supply of that metal as to merit attention. The report now communicated will inform you of their state and of the necessity of immediate inquiry into their occupation and titles.

With the Indian tribes established within our newly acquired limits, I have deemed it necessary to open conferences for the purpose of establishing a good understanding and neighborly relations between us. So far as we have yet learned, we have reason to believe that their dispositions are generally favorable and friendly; and with these dispositions on their part, we have in our own hands means which can not fail us for preserving their peace and friendship. By pursuing an uniform course of justice toward them, by aiding them in all the improvements which may better their condition, and especially by establishing a commerce on terms which shall be advantageous to them and only not losing to us, and so regulated as that no incendiaries of our own or any other nation may be permitted to disturb the natural effects of our just and friendly offices, we may render ourselves so necessary to their comfort and prosperity that the protection of our citizens from their disorderly members will become their interest and their voluntary care. Instead, therefore, of an augmentation of military force proportioned to our extension of frontier, I propose a moderate enlargement of the capital employed in that commerce as a more effectual, economical, and humane instrument for preserving peace and good neighborhood with them.

On this side of the Mississippi an important relinquishment of native title has been received from the Delawares. That tribe, desiring to extinguish in their people the spirit of hunting and to convert superfluous lands into the means of improving what they retain, has ceded to us all the country between the Wabash and Ohio south of and including the road from the rapids toward Vincennes, for which they are to receive annuities in animals and implements for agriculture and in other necessaries. This acquisition is important, not only for its extent and fertility, but as fronting three hundred miles on the Ohio, and near half that on the Wabash. The produce of the settled country descending those rivers will no longer pass in review of the Indian frontier but in a small portion, and, with the cession heretofore made by the Kaskaskias, nearly consolidates our possessions north of the Ohio, in a very respectable breadth—from Lake Erie to the Mississippi. The Piankeshaws having some claim to the country ceded by the Delawares, it has been thought best to quiet that by fair purchase also. So soon as the treaties on this subject shall have received their constitutional sanctions they shall be laid before both houses.

The act of Congress of February 28th, 1803, for building and employing a number of gun boats, is now in a course of execution to the extent there provided for. The obstacle to naval enterprise which vessels of this construction offer for our sea port towns, their utility toward supporting within our waters the authority of the laws, the promptness with which they will be manned by the sea men and militia of the place in the moment they are wanting, the facility of their assembling from different parts of the coast to any point where they are required in greater force than ordinary, the economy of their maintenance and preservation from decay when not in actual service, and the competence of our finances to this defensive provision without any new burthen are considerations which will have due weight with Congress in deciding on the expediency of adding to their number from year to year, as experience shall test their utility, until all our important harbors, by these and auxiliary means, shall be secured against insult and opposition to the laws.

No circumstance has arisen since your last session which calls for any augmentation of our regular military force. Should any improvement occur in the militia system, that will be always seasonable.

Accounts of the receipts and expenditures of the last year, with estimates for the ensuing one, will as usual be laid before you.

The state of our finances continues to fulfill our expectations. $11.5 millions, received in the course of the year ending the 30th of September last, have enabled us, after meeting all the ordinary expenses of the year, to pay upward of $3.6 millions of the public debt, exclusive of interest. This payment, with those of the two preceding years, has extinguished upward of $12 millions of the principal and a greater sum of interest within that period, and by a proportionate diminution of interest renders already sensible the effect of the growing sum yearly applicable to the discharge of the principal.

It is also ascertained that the revenue accrued during the last year exceeds that of the preceding, and the probable receipts of the ensuing year may safely be relied on as sufficient, with the sum already in the Treasury, to meet all the current demands of the year, to discharge upward of $3.5 millions of the engagements incurred under the British and French conventions, and to advance in the further redemption of the funded debt as rapidly as had been contemplated.

These, fellow citizens, are the principal matters which I have thought it necessary at this time to communicate for your consideration and attention. Some others will be laid before you in the course of the session; but in the discharge of the great duties confided to you by our country you will take a broader view of the field of legislation.

Whether the great interests of agriculture, manufactures, commerce, or navigation can within the pale of your constitutional powers be aided in any of their relations; whether laws are provided in all cases where they are wanting; whether those provided are exactly what they should be; whether any abuses take place in their administration, or in that of the public revenues; whether the organization of the public agents or of the public force is perfect in all its parts; in fine, whether anything can be done to advance the general good, are questions within the limits of your functions which will necessarily occupy your attention. In these and all other matters which you in your wisdom may propose for the good of our country, you may count with assurance on my hearty cooperation and faithful execution.

TH. JEFFERSON

# State of the Union Address

## *December 3, 1805*

The Senate and House of Representatives of the United States:

At a moment when the nations of Europe are in commotion and arming against each other, and when those with whom we have principal intercourse are engaged in the general contest, and when the countenance of some of them toward our peaceable country threatens that even that may not be unaffected by what is passing on the general theater, a meeting of the representatives of the nation in both Houses of Congress has become more than usually desirable. Coming from every section of our country, they bring with them the sentiments and the information of the whole, and will be enabled to give a direction to the public affairs which the will and the wisdom of the whole will approve and support.

In taking a view of the state of our country we in the first place notice the late affliction of two of our cities under the fatal fever which in latter times has occasionally visited our shores. Providence in His goodness gave it an early termination on this occasion and lessened the number of victims which have usually fallen before it. In the course of the several visitations by this disease it has appeared that it is strictly local, incident to cities and on the tide waters only, incommunicable in the country either by persons under the disease or by goods carried from diseased places; that its access is with the autumn and it disappears with the early frosts.

These restrictions within narrow limits of time and space give security even to our maritime cities during three quarter of the year, and to the country always. Although from these facts it appears unnecessary, yet to satisfy the fears of foreign nations and cautions on their part not to be complained of in a danger whose limits are yet unknown to them I have strictly enjoined on the officers at the head of the customs to certify with exact truth for every vessel sailing for a foreign port the state of health respecting this fever which prevails at the place from which she sails. Under every motive from character and duty to certify the truth, I have no doubt they have faithfully executed this injunction. Much real injury has, however, been sustained from a propensity to identify with this endemic and to call by the same name fevers of very different kinds, which have been known at all times and in all countries, and never have been placed among those deemed contagious.

As we advance in our knowledge of this disease, as facts develop the source from which individuals receive it, the State authorities charged with the care of the public health, and Congress with that of the general commerce, will become able to regulate with effect their respective functions in these departments. The burthen of quarantines is felt at home as well as abroad; their efficacy merits examination. Although the health laws of the States should be found to need no present revisal by Congress, yet commerce claims that their attention be ever awake to them.

Since our last meeting the aspect of our foreign relations has considerably changed. Our coasts have been infested and our harbors watched by private armed vessels, some of them without commissions, some with illegal commissions, others with those of legal form, but committing practical acts beyond the authority of their commissions. They have captured in the very entrance of our harbors, as well as on the high seas, not only the vessels of our friends coming to trade with us, but our own also. They have carried them off under pretense of legal adjudication, but not daring to approach a court of justice, they have plundered and sunk them by the way or in obscure places where no evidence could arise against them, maltreated the crews, and abandoned them in boats in the open sea or on desert shores without food or clothing. These enormities appearing to be unreached by any control of their sovereigns, I found it necessary to equip a force to cruise within our own seas, to arrest all vessels of these descriptions found hovering on our coasts within the limits of the Gulf Stream and to bring the offenders in for trial as pirates.

The same system of hovering on our coasts and harbors under color of seeking enemies has been also carried on by public armed ships to the great annoyance and oppression of our commerce. New principles, too, have been interpolated into the law of nations, founded neither in justice nor in the usage or acknowledgment of nations. According to these a belligerent takes to itself a commerce with its own enemy which it denies to a neutral on the ground of its aiding that enemy in the war; but reason revolts at such inconsistency, and the neutral having equal right with the belligerent to decide the question, the interests of our constituents and the duty of maintaining the authority of reason, the only umpire between just nations, impose on us the obligation of providing an effectual and determined opposition to a doctrine so injurious to the rights of peaceable nations. Indeed, the confidence we ought to have in the justice of others still countenances the hope that a sounder view of those rights will of itself induce from every belligerent a more correct observance of them.

With Spain our negotiations for a settlement of differences have not had a satisfactory issue. Spoliations during a former war, for which she had acknowledged herself responsible, have been refused to be compensated but on conditions affecting other claims in no wise connected with them. Yet the same practices are renewed in the present war and are already of great amount. On the Mobile, our commerce passing through that river continues to be obstructed by arbitrary duties and vexatious searches. Propositions for adjusting amicably the boundaries of Louisiana have not been acceded to. While, however, the right is unsettled, we have avoided changing the state of things by taking new posts or strengthening ourselves in the disputed territories, in the hope that the other power would not by a contrary conduct oblige us to meet their example and endanger conflicts of authority, the issue of which may not be easily controlled. But in this hope we have now reason to lessen our confidence.

Inroads have been recently made into the Territories of Orleans and the Mississippi, our citizens have been seized and their property plundered in the very parts of the former which had been actually delivered up by Spain, and this by the regular officers and soldiers of that Government. I have therefore found it necessary at length to give orders to our troops on that frontier to be in readiness to protect our citizens, and to repel by arms any similar aggressions in future. Other details necessary for your full information of the state of things between this country and that shall be the subject of another communication.

In reviewing these injuries from some of the belligerent powers the moderation, the firmness, and the wisdom of the Legislature will be called into action. We ought still to hope that time and a more correct estimate of interest as well as of character will produce the justice we are bound to expect, but should any nation deceive itself by false calculations, and disappoint that expectation, we must join in the unprofitable contest of trying which party can do the other the most harm.

Some of these injuries may perhaps admit a peaceable remedy. Where that is competent it is always the most desirable. But some of them are of a nature to be met by force only, and all of them may lead to it. I can not, therefore, but recommend such preparations as circumstances call for.

The first object is to place our sea port towns out of the danger of insult. Measures have been already taken for furnishing them with heavy cannon for the service of such land batteries as may make a part of their defense against armed vessels approaching them. In aid of these it is desirable we should have a competent number of gun boats, and the number, to be competent, must be considerable. If immediately begun, they may be in readiness for service at the opening of the next season.

Whether it will be necessary to augment our land forces will be decided by occurrences probably in the course of your session. In the mean time you will consider whether it would not be expedient for a state of peace as well as of war so to organize or class the militia as would enable us on any sudden emergency to call for the services of the younger portions, unencumbered with the old and those having families. Upward of three hundred thousand able-bodied men between the ages of 18 and 26 years, which the last census shews we may now count within our limits, will furnish a competent number for offense or defense in any point where they may be wanted, and will give time for raising regular forces after the necessity of them shall become certain; and the reducing to the early period of life all its active service can not but be desirable to our younger citizens of the present as well as future times, in as much as it engages to them in more advanced age a quiet and undisturbed repose in the bosom of their families. I can not, then, but earnestly recommend to your early consideration the expediency of so modifying our militia system as, by a separation of the more active part from that which is less so, we may draw from it when necessary an efficient corps fit for real and active service, and to be called to it in regular rotation.

Considerable provision has been made under former authorities from Congress of material for the construction of ships of war of 74 guns. These materials are on hand subject to the further will of the Legislature.

An immediate prohibition of the exportation of arms and ammunition is also submitted to your determination.

Turning from these unpleasant views of violence and wrong, I congratulate you on the liberation of our fellow citizens who were stranded on the coast of Tripoli and made prisoners of war. In a government bottomed on the will of all the life and liberty of every individual citizen become interesting to all.

In the treaty, therefore, which has concluded our warfare with that State an article for the ransom of our citizens has been agreed to. An operation by land by a small band of our country-men and others, engaged for the occasion in conjunction with the troops of the ex-Bashaw of that country, gallantly conducted by our late consul, Eaton, and their successful enterprise on the city of Derne, contributed doubtless to the impression which produced peace, and the conclusion of this prevented opportunities of which the officers and men of our squadron destined for Tripoli would have availed themselves to emulate the acts of valor exhibited by their brethren in the attack of the last year. Reflecting with high satisfaction on the distinguished bravery displayed whenever occasions permitted it in the late Mediterranean service, I think it would be an useful encouragement as well as a just reward to make an opening for some present promotion by enlarging our peace establishment of captains and lieutenants.

With Tunis some misunderstandings have arisen not yet sufficiently explained, but friendly discussions with their ambassador recently arrived and a mutual disposition to do whatever is just and reasonable can not fail of dissipating these, so that we may consider our peace on that coast, generally, to be on as sound a footing as it has been at any preceding time. Still, it will not be expedient to withdraw immediately the whole of our force from that sea.

The law providing for a naval peace establishment fixes the number of frigates which shall be kept in constant service in time of peace, and prescribes that they shall be manned by not more than two-thirds of their complement of sea men and ordinary sea men. Whether a frigate may be trusted to two-thirds only of her proper complement of men must depend on the nature of the service on which she is ordered; that may sometimes, for her safety as well as to insure her object, require her fullest complement. In adverting to this subject Congress will perhaps consider whether the best limitation on the Executive discretion in this case would not be by the number of sea men which may be employed in the whole service rather than by the number of vessels. Occasions oftener arise for the employment of small than of large vessels, and it would lessen risk as well as expense to be authorized to employ them of preference. The limitation suggested by the number of sea men would admit a selection of vessels best adapted to the service.

Our Indian neighbors are advancing, many of them with spirit, and others beginning to engage in the pursuits of agriculture and household manufacture. They are becoming sensible that the earth yields subsistence with less labor and more certainty than the forest, and find it their interest from time to time to dispose of parts of their surplus and waste lands for the means of improving those they occupy and of subsisting their families while they are preparing their farms. Since your last session the Northern tribes have sold to us the lands between the Connecticut Reserve and the former Indian boundary and those on the Ohio from the same boundary to the rapids and for a considerable depth inland. The Chickasaws and Cherokees have sold us the country between and adjacent to the two districts of Tennessee, and the Creeks the residue of their lands in the fork of the Ocmulgee up to the Ulcofauhatche. The three former purchases are important, in as much as they consolidate disjoined parts of our settled country and render their intercourse secure; and the second particularly so, as, with the small point on the river which we expect is by this time ceded by the Piankeshaws, it completes our possession of the whole of both banks of the Ohio from its source to near its mouth, and the navigation of that river is thereby rendered forever safe to our citizens settled and settling on its extensive waters. The purchase from the Creeks, too, has been for some time particularly interesting to the State of Georgia.

The several treaties which have been mentioned will be submitted to both
Houses of Congress for the exercise of their respective functions.

Deputations now on their way to the seat of Government from various nations of Indians inhabiting the Missouri and other parts beyond the Mississippi come charged with assurances of their satisfaction with the new relations in which they are placed with us, of their dispositions to cultivate our peace and friendship, and their desire to enter into commercial intercourse with us. A state of our progress in exploring the principal rivers of that country, and of the information respecting them hitherto obtained, will be communicated as soon as we shall receive some further relations which we have reason shortly to expect.

The receipts of the Treasury during the year ending on the 30th day of September last have exceeded the sum of $13 millions, which, with not quite $5 millions in the Treasury at the beginning of the year, have enabled us after meeting other demands to pay nearly $2 millions of the debt contracted under the British treaty and convention, upward of $4 millions of principal of the public debt, and $4 millions of interest. These payments, with those which had been made in three years and a half preceding, have extinguished of the funded debt nearly $18 millions of principal. Congress by their act of November 10th, 1803, authorized us to borrow $1.75 millions toward meeting the claims of our citizens assumed by the convention with France. We have not, however, made use of this authority, because the sum of $4.5 millions, which remained in the Treasury on the same 30th day of September last, with the receipts of which we may calculate on for the ensuing year, besides paying the annual sum of $8 millions appropriated to the funded debt and meeting all the current demands which may be expected, will enable us to pay the whole sum of $3.75 millions assumed by the French convention and still leave us a surplus of nearly $1 million at our free disposal. Should you concur in the provisions of arms and armed vessels recommended by the circumstances of the times, this surplus will furnish the means of doing so.

On this first occasion of addressing Congress since, by the choice of my constituents, I have entered on a second term of administration, I embrace the opportunity to give this public assurance that I will exert my best endeavors to administer faithfully the executive department, and will zealously cooperate with you in every measure which may tend to secure the liberty, property, and personal safety of our fellow citizens, and to consolidate the republican forms and principles of our Government.

In the course of your session you shall receive all the aid which I can give for the dispatch of public business, and all the information necessary for your deliberations, of which the interests of our own country and the confidence reposed in us by others will admit a communication.

TH. JEFFERSON

# State of the Union Address

## *December 2, 1806*

The Senate and House of Representatives of the United States:

It would have given me, fellow citizens, great satisfaction to announce in the moment of your meeting that the difficulties in our foreign relations existing at the time of your last separation had been amicably and justly terminated. I lost no time in taking those measures which were most likely to bring them to such a termination—by special missions charged with such powers and instructions as in the event of failure could leave no imputation on either our moderation or forbearance. The delays which have since taken place in our negotiations with the British Government appear to have proceeded from causes which do not forbid the expectation that during the course of the session I may be enabled to lay before you their final issue. What will be that of the negotiations for settling our differences with Spain nothing which had taken place at the date of the last dispatches enables us to pronounce. On the western side of the Mississippi she advanced in considerable force, and took post at the settlement of Bayou Pierre, on the Red River. This village was originally settled by France, was held by her as long as she held Louisiana, and was delivered to Spain only as a part of Louisiana. Being small, insulated, and distant, it was not observed at the moment of redelivery to France and the United States that she continued a guard of half a dozen men which had been stationed there. A proposition, however, having been lately made by our commander in chief to assume the Sabine River as a temporary line of separation between the troops of the two nations until the issue of our negotiations shall be known, this has been referred by the Spanish commandant to his superior, and in the mean time he has withdrawn his force to the western side of the Sabine River. The correspondence on this subject now communicated will exhibit more particularly the present state of things in that quarter.

The nature of that country requires indispensably that an unusual proportion of the force employed there should be cavalry or mounted infantry. In order, therefore, that the commanding officer might be enabled to act with effect, I had authorized him to call on the governors of Orleans and Mississippi for a corps of five hundred volunteer cavalry. The temporary arrangement he has proposed may perhaps render this unnecessary; but I inform you with great pleasure of the promptitude with which the inhabitants of those Territories have tendered their services in defense of their country. It has done honor to themselves, entitled them to the confidence of their fellow citizens in every part of the Union, and must strengthen the general determination to protect them efficaciously under all circumstances which may occur.

Having received information that in another part of the United States a great number of private individuals were combining together, arming and organizing themselves contrary to law, to carry on a military expedition against the territories of Spain, I thought it necessary, by proclamation as well as by special orders, to take measures for preventing and suppressing this enterprise, for seizing the vessels, arms, and other means provided for it, and for arresting and bringing to justice its authors and abettors. It was due to that good faith which ought ever to be the rule of action in public as well as in private transactions, it was due to good order and regular government, that while the public force was acting strictly on defensive and merely to protect our citizens from aggression the criminal attempts of private individuals to decide for their country the question of peace or war by commencing active and unauthorized hostilities should be promptly and efficaciously suppressed.

Whether it will be necessary to enlarge our regular forces will depend on the result of our negotiations with Spain; but as it is uncertain when that result will be known, the provisional measures requisite for that, and to meet any pressure intervening in that quarter, will be a subject for your early consideration.

The possession of both banks of the Mississippi reducing to a single point the defense of that river, its waters, and the country adjacent, it becomes highly necessary to provide for that point a more adequate security. Some position above its mouth, commanding the passage of the river, should be rendered sufficiently strong to cover the armed vessels which may be stationed there for defense, and in conjunction with them to present an insuperable obstacle to any force attempting to pass. The approaches to the city of New Orleans from the eastern quarter also will require to be examined and more effectually guarded. For the internal support of the country the encouragement of a strong settlement on the western side of the Mississippi, within reach of New Orleans, will be worthy the consideration of the Legislature.

The gun boats authorized by an act of the last session are so advanced that they will be ready for service in the ensuing spring. Circumstances permitted us to allow the time necessary for their more solid construction. As a much larger number will still be wanting to place our sea port towns and waters in that state of defense to which we are competent and they entitled, a similar appropriation for a further provision for them is recommended for the ensuing year.

A further appropriation will also be necessary for repairing fortifications already established and the erection of such other works as may have real effect in obstructing the approach of an enemy to our sea port towns, or their remaining before them.

In a country whose constitution is derived from the will of the people, directly expressed by their free suffrages; where the principal executive functionaries and those of the legislature are renewed by them at short periods; where under the character of jurors they exercise in person the greatest portion of the judiciary powers; where the laws are consequently so formed and administered as to bear with equal weight and favor on all, restraining no man in the pursuits of honest industry and securing to everyone the property which that acquires, it would not be supposed that any safe-guards could be needed against insurrection or enterprise on the public peace or authority. The laws, however, aware that these should not be trusted to moral restraints only, have wisely provided punishment for these crimes when committed. But would it not be salutary to give also the means of preventing their commission? Where an enterprise is meditated by private individuals against a foreign nation in amity with the United States, powers of prevention to a certain extent are given by the laws. Would they not be as reasonable and useful where the enterprise preparing is against the United States? While adverting to this branch of law it is proper to observe that in enterprises meditated against foreign nations the ordinary process of binding to the observance of the peace and good behavior, could it be extended to acts to be done out of the jurisdiction of the United States, would be effectual in some cases where the offender is able to keep out of sight every indication of his purpose which could draw on him the exercise of the powers now given by law.

The States on the coast of Barbary seem generally disposed at present to respect our peace and friendship; with Tunis alone some uncertainty remains. Persuaded that it is our interest to maintain our peace with them on equal terms or not at all, I propose to send in due time a reenforcement into the Mediterranean unless previous information shall show it to be unnecessary.

We continue to receive proofs of the growing attachment of our Indian neighbors and of their dispositions to place all their interests under the patronage of the United States. These dispositions are inspired by their confidence in our justice and in the sincere concern we feel for their welfare; and as long as we discharge these high and honorable functions with the integrity and good faith which alone can entitle us to their continuance we may expect to reap the just reward in their peace and friendship.

The expedition of Messrs. Lewis and Clarke for exploring the river Missouri and the best communication from that to the Pacific Ocean has had all the success which could have been expected. They have traced the Missouri nearly to its source, descended the Columbia to the Pacific Ocean, ascertained with accuracy the geography of that interesting communication across our continent, learnt the character of the country, of its commerce and inhabitants; and it is but justice to say that Messrs. Lewis and Clarke and their brave companions have by this arduous service deserved well of their country.

The attempt to explore the Red River, under the direction of Mr. Freeman, though conducted with a zeal and prudence meriting entire approbation, has not been equally successful. After proceeding up it about six hundred miles, nearly as far as the French settlements had extended while the country was in their possession, our geographers were obliged to return without completing their work.

Very useful additions have also been made to our knowledge of the Mississippi by Lieutenant Pike, who has ascended it to its source, and whose journal and map, giving the details of his journey, will shortly be ready for communication to both Houses of Congress. Those of Messrs. Lewis, Clarke, and Freeman will require further time to be digested and prepared. These important surveys, in addition to those before possessed, furnish materials for commencing an accurate map of the Mississippi and its western waters. Some principal rivers, however, remain still to be explored, toward which the authorization of Congress by moderate appropriations will be requisite.

I congratulate you, fellow citizens, on the approach of the period at which you may interpose your authority constitutionally to withdraw the citizens of the United States from all further participation in those violations of human rights which have been so long continued on the unoffending inhabitants of Africa, and which the morality, the reputation, and the best of our country have long been eager to proscribe. Although no law you may pass can take prohibitory effect until the first day of the year 1808, yet the intervening period is not too long to prevent by timely notice expeditions which can not be completed before that day.

The receipts at the Treasury during the year ending on the 30th day of September last have amounted to near $15 millions, which have enabled us, after meeting the current demands, to pay $2.7 millions of the American claims in part of the price of Louisiana; to pay of the funded debt upward of $3 millions of principal and nearly $4 millions of interest, and, in addition, to reimburse in the course of the present month near $2 millions of 5.5% stock. These payments and reimbursements of the funded debt, with those which had been made in the four years and a half preceding, will at the close of the present year have extinguished upward of $23 millions of principal.

The duties composing the Mediterranean fund will cease by law at the end of the present session. Considering, however, that they are levied chiefly on luxuries and that we have an impost on salt, a necessary of life, the free use of which otherwise is so important, I recommend to your consideration the suppression of the duties on salt and the continuation of the Mediterranean fund instead thereof for a short time, after which that also will become unnecessary for any purpose now within contemplation.

When both of these branches of revenue shall in this way be relinquished there will still ere long be an accumulation of moneys in the Treasury beyond the installments of public debt which we are permitted by contract to pay. They can not then, without a modification assented to by the public creditors, be applied to the extinguishment of this debt and the complete liberation of our revenues, the most desirable of all objects. Nor, if our peace continues, will they be wanting for any other existing purpose. The question therefore now comes forward, To what other objects shall these surpluses be appropriated, and the whole surplus of impost, after the entire discharge of the public debt, and during those intervals when the purposes of war shall not call for them? Shall we suppress the impost and give that advantage to foreign over domestic manufactures? On a few articles of more general and necessary use the suppression in due season will doubtless be right, but the great mass of the articles on which impost is paid are foreign luxuries, purchased by those only who are rich enough to afford themselves the use of them.

Their patriotism would certainly prefer its continuance and application to the great purposes of the public education, roads, rivers, canals, and such other objects of public improvement as it may be thought proper to add to the constitutional enumeration of Federal powers. By these operations new channels of communications will be opened between the States, the lines of separation will disappear, their interests will be identified, and their union cemented by new and indissoluble ties. Education is here placed among the articles of public care, not that it would be proposed to take its ordinary branches out of the hands of private enterprise, which manages so much better all the concerns to which it is equal, but a public institution can alone supply those sciences which though rarely called for are yet necessary to complete the circle, all the parts of which contribute to the improvement of the country and some of them to its preservation.

The subject is now proposed for the consideration of Congress, because if approved by the time the State legislatures shall have deliberated on this extension of the Federal trusts, and the laws shall be passed and other arrangements made for their execution, the necessary funds will be on hand and without employment.

I suppose an amendment to the Constitution, by consent of the States, necessary, because the objects now recommended are not among those enumerated in the Constitution, and to which it permits the public moneys to be applied.

The present consideration of a national establishment for education particularly is rendered proper by this circumstance also, that if Congress, approving the proposition, shall yet think it more eligible to found it on a donation of lands, they have it now in their power to endow it with those which will be among the earliest to produce the necessary income. This foundation would have the advantage of being independent of war, which may suspend other improvements by requiring for its own purposes the resources destined for them.

This, fellow citizens, is the state of the public interests at the present moment and according to the information now possessed. But such is the situation of the nations of Europe and such, too, the predicament in which we stand with some of them that we can not rely with certainty on the present aspect of our affairs, that may change from moment to moment during the course of your session or after you shall have separated.

Our duty is, therefore, to act upon things as they are and to make a reasonable provision for whatever they may be. Were armies to be raised whenever a speck of war is visible in our horizon, we never should have been without them. Our resources would have been exhausted on dangers which have never happened, instead of being reserved for what is really to take place. A steady, perhaps a quickened, pace in preparation for the defense of our sea port towns and waters; an early settlement of the most exposed and vulnerable parts of our country; a militia so organized that its effective portions can be called to any point in the Union, or volunteers instead of them to serve a sufficient time, are means which may always be ready, yet never preying on our resources until actually called into use. They will maintain the public interests while a more permanent force shall be in course of preparation. But much will depend on the promptitude with which these means can be brought into activity. If war be forced upon us, in spite of our long and vain appeals to the justice of nations, rapid and vigorous movements in its outset will go far toward securing us in its course and issue, and toward throwing its burthens on those who render necessary the resort from reason to force.

The result of our negotiations, or such incidents in their course as may enable us to infer their probable issue; such further movements also on our western frontiers as may shew whether war is to be pressed there while negotiation is protracted elsewhere, shall be communicated to you from time to time as they become known to me, with whatever other information I possess or may receive, which may aid your deliberations on the great national interests committed to your charge.

TH. JEFFERSON

# State of the Union Address

## *October 27, 1807*

The Senate and House of Representatives of the United States:

Circumstances, fellow citizens, which seriously threatened the peace of our country have made it a duty to convene you at an earlier period than usual. The love of peace so much cherished in the bosoms of our citizens, which has so long guided the proceedings of their public councils and induced forbearance under so many wrongs, may not insure our continuance in the quiet pursuits of industry. The many injuries and depredations committed on our commerce and navigation upon the high seas for years past, the successive innovations on those principles of public law which have been established by the reason and usage of nations as the rule of their intercourse and the umpire and security of their rights and peace, and all the circumstances which induced the extraordinary mission to London are already known to you.

The instructions given to our ministers were framed in the sincerest spirit of amity and moderation. They accordingly proceeded, in conformity therewith, to propose arrangements which might embrace and settle all the points in difference between us, which might bring us to a mutual understanding on our neutral and national rights and provide for a commercial intercourse on conditions of some equality. After long and fruitless endeavors to effect the purposes of their mission and to obtain arrangements within the limits of their instructions, they concluded to sign such as could be obtained and to send them for consideration, candidly declaring to the other negotiators at the same time that they were acting against their instructions, and that their Government, therefore, could not be pledged for ratification.

Some of the articles proposed might have been admitted on a principle of compromise, but others were too highly disadvantageous, and no sufficient provision was made against the principal source of the irritations and collisions which were constantly endangering the peace of the two nations. The question, therefore, whether a treaty should be accepted in that form could have admitted but of one decision, even had no declarations of the other party impaired our confidence in it. Still anxious not to close the door against friendly adjustment, new modifications were framed and further concessions authorized than could before have been supposed necessary; and our ministers were instructed to resume their negotiations on these grounds.

On this new reference to amicable discussion we were reposing in confidence, when on the 22nd day of June last by a formal order from a British admiral the frigate Chesapeake, leaving her port for a distant service, was attacked by one of those vessels which had been lying in our harbors under the indulgences of hospitality, was disabled from proceeding, had several of her crew killed and four taken away. On this outrage no commentaries are necessary. Its character has been pronounced by the indignant voices of our citizens with an emphasis and unanimity never exceeded. I immediately, by proclamation, interdicted our harbors and waters to all British armed vessels, forbade intercourse with them, and uncertain how far hostilities were intended, and the town of Norfolk, indeed, being threatened with immediate attack, a sufficient force was ordered for the protection of that place, and such other preparations commenced and pursued as the prospect rendered proper. An armed vessel of the United States was dispatched with instructions to our ministers at London to call on that Government for the satisfaction and security required by the outrage. A very short interval ought now to bring the answer, which shall be communicated to you as soon as received; then also, or as soon after as the public interests shall be found to admit, the unratified treaty and proceedings relative to it shall be made known to you.

The aggression thus begun has been continued on the part of the British commanders by remaining within our waters in defiance of the authority of the country, by habitual violations of its jurisdiction, and at length by putting to death one of the persons whom they had forcibly taken from on board the Chesapeake. These aggravations necessarily lead to the policy either of never admitting an armed vessel into our harbors or of maintaining in every harbor such an armed force as may constrain obedience to the laws and protect the lives and property of our citizens against their armed guests; but the expense of such a standing force and its inconsistence with our principles dispense with those courtesies which would necessarily call for it, and leave us equally free to exclude the navy, as we are the army, of a foreign power from entering our limits.

To former violations of maritime rights another is now added of very extensive effect. The Government of that nation has issued an order interdicting all trade by neutrals between ports not in amity with them; and being now at war with nearly every nation on the Atlantic and Mediterranean seas, our vessels are required to sacrifice their cargoes at the first port they touch or to return home without the benefit of going to any other market. Under this new law of the ocean our trade on the Mediterranean has been swept away by seizures and condemnations, and that in other seas is threatened with the same fate.

Our differences with Spain remain still unsettled, no measure having been taken on her part since my last communications to Congress to bring them to a close. But under a state of things which may favor reconsideration they have been recently pressed, and an expectation is entertained that they may now soon be brought to an issue of some sort. With their subjects on our borders no new collisions have taken place nor seem immediately to be apprehended. To our former grounds of complaint has been added a very serious one, as you will see by the decree a copy of which is now communicated. Whether this decree, which professes to be conformable to that of the French Government of November 21st, 1806, heretofore communicated to Congress, will also be conformed to that in its construction and application in relation to the United States had not been ascertained at the date of our last communications. These, however, gave reason to expect such a conformity.

With the other nations of Europe our harmony has been uninterrupted, and commerce and friendly intercourse have been maintained on their usual footing.

Our peace with the several states on the coast of Barbary appears as firm as at any former period and as likely to continue as that of any other nation.

Among our Indian neighbors in the northwestern quarter some fermentation was observed soon after the late occurrences, threatening the continuance of our peace. Messages were said to be interchanged and tokens to be passing, which usually denote a state of restless among them, and the character of the agitators pointed to the sources of excitement. Measures were immediately taken for providing against that danger; instructions were given to require explanations, and, with assurances of our continued friendship, to admonish the tribes to remain quiet at home, taking no part in quarrels not belonging to them. As far as we are yet informed, the tribes in our vicinity, who are most advanced in the pursuits of industry, are sincerely disposed to adhere to their friendship with us and to their peace with all others, while those more remote do not present appearances sufficiently quiet to justify the intermission of military precaution on our part.

The great tribes on our southwestern quarter, much advanced beyond the others in agriculture and household arts, appear tranquil and identifying their views with ours in proportion to their advancement. With the whole of these people, in every quarter, I shall continue to inculcate peace and friendship with all their neighbors and perseverance in those occupations and pursuits which will best promote their own well-being.

The appropriations of the last session for the defense of our sea port towns and harbors were made under expectation that a continuance of our peace would permit us to proceed in that work according to our convenience. It has been thought better to apply the sums then given toward the defense of New York, Charleston, and New Orleans chiefly, as most open and most likely first to need protection, and to leave places less immediately in danger to the provisions of the present session.

The gun boats, too, already provided have on a like principle been chiefly assigned to New York, New Orleans, and the Chesapeake. Whether our movable force on the water, so material in aid of the defensive works on the land, should be augmented in this or any other form is left to the wisdom of the Legislature. For the purpose of manning these vessels in sudden attacks on our harbors it is a matter for consideration whether the sea men of the United States may not justly be formed into a special militia, to be called on for tours of duty in defense of the harbors where they shall happen to be, the ordinary militia of the place furnishing that portion which may consist of landsmen.

The moment our peace was threatened I deemed it indispensable to secure a greater provision of those articles of military stores with which our magazines were not sufficiently furnished. To have awaited a previous and special sanction by law would have lost occasions which might not be retrieved. I did not hesitate, therefore, to authorize engagements for such supplements to our existing stock as would render it adequate to the emergencies threatening us, and I trust that the Legislature, feeling the same anxiety for the safety of our country, so materially advanced by this precaution, will approve, when done, what they would have seen so important to be done if then assembled. Expenses, also unprovided for, arose out of the necessity of calling all our gun boats into actual service for the defense of our harbors; all of which accounts will be laid before you.

Whether a regular army is to be raised, and to what extent, must depend on the information so shortly expected. In the mean time I have called on the States for quotas of militia, to be in readiness for present defense, and have, moreover, encouraged the acceptance of volunteers; and I am happy to inform you that these have offered themselves with great alacrity in every part of the Union. They are ordered to be organized and ready at a moment's warning to proceed on any service to which they may be called, and every preparation within the Executive powers has been made to insure us the benefit of early exertions.

I informed Congress at their last session of the enterprises against the public peace which were believed to be in preparation by Aaron Burr and his associates, of the measures taken to defeat them and to bring the offenders to justice. Their enterprises were happily defeated by the patriotic exertions of the militia whenever called into action, by the fidelity of the Army, and energy of the commander in chief in promptly arranging the difficulties presenting themselves on the Sabine, repairing to meet those arising on the Mississippi, and dissipating before their explosion plots engendering there. I shall think it my duty to lay before you the proceedings and the evidence publicly exhibited on the arraignment of the principal offenders before the circuit court of Virginia.

You will be enabled to judge whether the defect was in the testimony, in the law, or in the administration of the law; and wherever it shall be found, the Legislature alone can apply or originate the remedy. The framers of our Constitution certainly supposed they had guarded as well their Government against destruction by treason as their citizens against oppression under pretense of it, and if these ends are not attained it is of importance to inquire by what means more effectual they may be secured.

The accounts of the receipts of revenue during the year ending on the 30th day of September last being not yet made up, a correct statement will be hereafter transmitted from the Treasury. In the mean time, it is ascertained that the receipts have amounted to near $16 millions, which, with the $5.5 millions in the Treasury at the beginning of the year, have enabled us, after meeting the current demands and interest incurred, to pay more than $4 millions of the principal of our funded debt. These payments, with those of the preceding five and a half years, have extinguished of the funded debt $25.5 millions, being the whole which could be paid or purchased within the limits of the law and of our contracts, and have left us in the Treasury $8.5 millions.

A portion of this sum may be considered as a commencement of accumulation of the surpluses of revenue which, after paying the installments of debt as they shall become payable, will remain without any specific object. It may partly, indeed, be applied toward completing the defense of the exposed points of our country, on such a scale as shall be adapted to our principles and circumstances. This object is doubtless among the first entitled to attention in such a state of our finances, and it is one which, whether we have peace or war, will provide security where it is due. Whether what shall remain of this, with the future surpluses, may be usefully applied to purposes already authorized or more usefully to others requiring new authorities, or how otherwise they shall be disposed of, are questions calling for the notice of Congress, unless, indeed, they shall be superseded by a change in our public relations now awaiting the determination of others. Whatever be that determination, it is a great consolation that it will become known at a moment when the supreme council of the nation is assembled at its post, and ready to give the aids of its wisdom and authority to whatever course the good of our country shall then call us to pursue.

Matters of minor importance will be the subjects of future communications, and nothing shall be wanting on my part which may give information or dispatch to the proceedings of the Legislature in the exercise of their high duties, and at a moment so interesting to the public welfare.

TH. JEFFERSON

# State of the Union Address

## *November 8, 1808*

The Senate and House of Representatives of the United States:

It would have been a source, fellow citizens, of much gratification if our last communications from Europe had enabled me to inform you that the belligerent nations, whose disregard of neutral rights has been so destructive to our commerce, had become awakened to the duty and true policy of revoking their unrighteous edicts. That no means might be omitted to produce this salutary effect, I lost no time in availing myself of the act authorizing a suspension, in whole or in part, of the several embargo laws. Our ministers at London and Paris were instructed to explain to the respective Governments there our disposition to exercise the authority in such manner as would withdraw the pretext on which the aggressions were originally founded and open the way for a renewal of that commercial intercourse which it was alleged on all sides had been reluctantly obstructed.

As each of those Governments had pledged its readiness to concur in renouncing a measure which reached its adversary through the incontestable rights of neutrals only, and as the measure had been assumed by each as a retaliation for an asserted acquiescence in the aggression of the other, it was reasonably expected that the occasion would have been seized by both for evincing the sincerity of their professions, and for restoring to the commerce of the United States its legitimate freedom. The instructions to our ministers with respect to the different belligerents were necessarily modified with a reference to their different circumstances, and to the condition annexed by law to the Executive power of suspension, requiring a decree of security to our commerce which would not result from a repeal of the decrees of France. Instead of a pledge, therefore, of a suspension of the embargo as to her in case of such a repeal, it was presumed that a sufficient inducement might be found in other considerations, and particularly in the change produced by a compliance with our just demands by one belligerent and a refusal by the other in the relations between the other and the United States.

To Great Britain, whose power on the ocean is so ascendant, it was deemed not inconsistent with that condition to state explicitly that on her rescinding her orders in relation to the United States their trade would be opened with her, and remain shut to her enemy in case of his failure to rescind his decrees also. From France no answer has been received, nor any indication that the requisite change in her decrees is contemplated. The favorable reception of the proposition to Great Britain was the less to be doubted, as her orders of council had not only been referred for their vindication to an acquiescence on the part of the United States no longer to be pretended, but as the arrangement proposed, whilst it resisted the illegal decrees of France, involved, moreover, substantially the precise advantages professedly aimed at by the British orders. The arrangement has nevertheless been rejected.

This candid and liberal experiment having thus failed, and no other event having occurred on which a suspension of the embargo by the Executive was authorized, it necessarily remains in the extent originally given to it. We have the satisfaction, however, to reflect that in return for the privations imposed by the measure, and which our fellow citizens in general have borne with patriotism, it has had the important effects of saving our mariners and our vast mercantile property, as well as of affording time for prosecuting the defensive and provisional measures called for by the occasion. It has demonstrated to foreign nations the moderation and firmness which govern our councils, and to our citizens the necessity of uniting in support of the laws and the rights of their country, and has thus long frustrated those usurpations and spoliations which, if resisted, involved war; if submitted to, sacrificed a vital principle of our national independence.

Under a continuance of the belligerent measures which, in defiance of laws which consecrate the rights of neutrals, overspread the ocean with danger, it will rest with the wisdom of Congress to decide on the course best adapted to such a state of things; and bringing with them, as they do, from every part of the Union the sentiments of our constituents, my confidence is strengthened that in forming this decision they will, with an unerring regard to the essential rights and interests of the nation, weigh and compare the painful alternatives out of which a choice is to be made. Nor should I do justice to the virtues which on other occasions have marked the character of our fellow citizens if I did not cherish an equal confidence that the alternative chosen, whatever it may be, will be maintained with all the fortitude and patriotism which the crisis ought to inspire.

The documents containing the correspondences on the subject of the foreign edicts against our commerce, with the instructions given to our ministers at London and Paris, are now laid before you.

The communications made to Congress at their last session explained the posture in which the close of the discussions relating to the attack by a British ship of war on the frigate

Chesapeake left a subject on which the nation had manifested so honorable a sensibility. Every view of what had passed authorized a belief that immediate steps would be taken by the British Government for redressing a wrong which the more it was investigated appeared the more clearly to require what had not been provided for in the special mission. It is found that no steps have been taken for the purpose. On the contrary, it will be seen in the documents laid before you that the inadmissible preliminary which obstructed the adjustment is still adhered to, and, moreover, that it is now brought into connection with the distinct and irrelative case of the orders in council. The instructions which had been given to our minister at London with a view to facilitate, if necessary, the reparation claimed by the United States are included in the documents communicated.

Our relations with the other powers of Europe have undergone no material changes since your last session. The important negotiations with Spain which had been alternately suspended and resumed necessarily experience a pause under the extraordinary and interesting crisis which distinguishes her internal situation.

With the Barbary Powers we continue in harmony, with the exception of an unjustifiable proceeding of the Dey of Algiers toward our consul to that Regency. Its character and circumstances are now laid before you, and will enable you to decide how far it may, either now or hereafter, call for any measures not within the limits of the Executive authority.

With our Indian neighbors the public peace has been steadily maintained. Some instances of individual wrong have, as at other times, taken place, but in no wise implicating the will of the nation. Beyond the Mississippi the Ioways, the Sacs and the Alabamas have delivered up for trial and punishment individuals from among themselves accused of murdering citizens of the United States. On this side of the Mississippi the Creeks are exerting themselves to arrest offenders of the same kind, and the Choctaws have manifested their readiness and desire for amicable and just arrangements respecting depredations committed by disorderly persons of their tribe. And, generally, from a conviction that we consider them as a part of ourselves, and cherish with sincerity their rights and interests, the attachment of the Indian tribes is gaining strength daily—is extending from the nearer to the more remote, and will amply requite us for the justice and friendship practiced toward them. Husbandry and household manufacture are advancing among them more rapidly with the Southern than Northern tribes, from circumstances of soil and climate, and one of the two great divisions of the Cherokee Nation have now under consideration to solicit the citizenship of the United States, and to be identified with us in laws and government in such progressive manner as we shall think best.

In consequence of the appropriations of the last session of Congress for the security of our sea port towns and harbors, such works of defense have been erected as seemed to be called for by the situation of the several places, their relative importance, and the scale of expense indicated by the amount of the appropriation. These works will chiefly be finished in the course of the present season, except at New York and New Orleans, where most was to be done; and although a great proportion of the last appropriation has been expended on the former place, yet some further views will be submitted to Congress for rendering its security entirely adequate against naval enterprise. A view of what has been done at the several places, and of what is proposed to be done, shall be communicated as soon as the several reports are received.

Of the gun boats authorized by the act of December last, it has been thought necessary to build only one hundred and three in the present year. These, with those before possessed, are sufficient for the harbors and waters most exposed, and the residents will require little time for their construction when it shall be deemed necessary.

Under the act of the last session for raising an additional military force so many officers were immediately appointed as were necessary for carrying on the business of recruiting, and in proportion as it advanced others have been added. We have reason to believe their success has been satisfactory, although such returns have not yet been received as enable me to present you a statement of the numbers engaged.

I have not thought it necessary in the course of the last season to call for any general detachments of militia or of volunteers under the laws passed for that purpose. For the ensuing season, however, they will be required to be in readiness should their service be wanted. Some small and special detachments have been necessary to maintain the laws of embargo on that portion of our northern frontier which offered peculiar facilities for evasion, but these were replaced as soon as it could be done by bodies of new recruits. By the aid of these and of the armed vessels called into service in other quarters the spirit of disobedience and abuse, which manifested itself early and with sensible effect while we were unprepared to meet it, has been considerably repressed.
Considering the extraordinary character of the times in which we live, our attention should unremittingly be fixed on the safety of our country. For a people who are free, and

who mean to remain so, a well organized and armed militia is their best security. It is therefore incumbent on us at every meeting to revise the condition of the militia, and to ask ourselves if it is prepared to repel a powerful enemy at every point of our territories exposed to invasion. Some of the States have paid a laudable attention to this object, but every degree of neglect is to be found among others. Congress alone having the power to produce an uniform state of preparation in this great organ of defense, the interests which they so deeply feel in their own and their country's security will present this as among the most important objects of their deliberation.

Under the acts of March 11th and April 23rd respecting arms, the difficulty of procuring them from abroad during the present situation and dispositions of Europe induced us to direct our whole efforts to the means of internal supply. The public factories have therefore been enlarged, additional machineries erected, and, in proportion as artificers can be found or formed, their effect, already more than doubled, may be increased so as to keep pace with the yearly increase of the militia. The annual sums appropriated by the latter have been directed to the encouragement of private factories of arms, and contracts have been entered into with individual undertakers to nearly the amount of the first year's appropriation.

The suspension of our foreign commerce, produced by the injustice of the belligerent powers and the consequent losses and sacrifices of our citizens are subjects of just concern. The situation into which we have thus been forced has impelled us to apply a portion of our industry and capital to internal manufactures and improvements. The extent of this conversion is daily increasing, and little doubt remains that the establishments formed and forming will, under the auspices of cheaper materials and subsistence, the freedom of labor from taxation with us, and of protecting duties and prohibitions, become permanent. The commerce with the Indians, too, within our own boundaries is likely to receive abundant aliment from the same internal source, and will secure to them peace and the progress of civilization, undisturbed by practices hostile to both.

The accounts of the receipts and expenditures during the year ending the 30th of September last being not yet made up, a correct statement will hereafter be transmitted from the Treasury. In the mean time it is ascertained that the receipts have amounted to near $18 millions, which, with the $8.5 millions in the Treasury at the beginning of the year, have enabled us, after meeting the current demands and interest incurred, to pay $2.3 millions of the principal of our funded debt, and left us in the Treasury on that day near $14 millions. Of these, $5.35 millions will be necessary to pay what will be due on the 1st day of January next, which will complete the reimbursement of the 8% stock. These payments, with those made in the six and a half years preceding, will have extinguished $33.58 millions of the principal of the funded debt, being the whole which could be paid or purchased within the limits of the law and of our contracts, and the amount of principal thus discharged will have liberated the revenue from about $2 millions of interest and added that sum annually to the disposable surplus.

The probable accumulation of the surpluses of revenue beyond what can be applied to the payment of the public debt whenever the freedom and safety of our commerce shall be restored merits the consideration of Congress. Shall it lie unproductive in the public vaults? Shall the revenue be reduced? Or shall it not rather be appropriated to the improvements of roads, canals, rivers, education, and other great foundations of prosperity and union under the powers which Congress may already possess or such amendment to the Constitution as may be approved by the States? While uncertain of the course of things, the time may be advantageously employed in obtaining the powers necessary for a system of improvement, should that be thought best.

Availing myself of this the last occasion which will occur of addressing the two Houses of the Legislature at their meeting, I can not omit the expression of my sincere gratitude for the repeated proofs of confidence manifested to me by themselves and their predecessors since my call to the administration and the many indulgences experienced at their hands. These same grateful acknowledgements are due to my fellow citizens generally, whose support has been my great encouragement under all embarrassments. In the transaction of their business I can not have escaped error. It is incident to our imperfect nature. But I may say with truth my errors have been of the understanding, not of intention, and that the advancement of their rights and interests has been the constant motive for every measure. On these considerations I solicit their indulgence. Looking forward with anxiety to future destinies, I trust that in their steady character, unshaken by difficulties, in their love of liberty, obedience to law, and support of the public authorities, I see a sure guaranty of the permanence of our Republic; and, retiring from the charge of their affairs, I carry with me the consolation of a firm persuasion that Heaven has in store for our beloved country long ages to come of prosperity and happiness.

TH. JEFFERSON

Made in the USA
Lexington, KY
07 March 2014